LOUISIANA

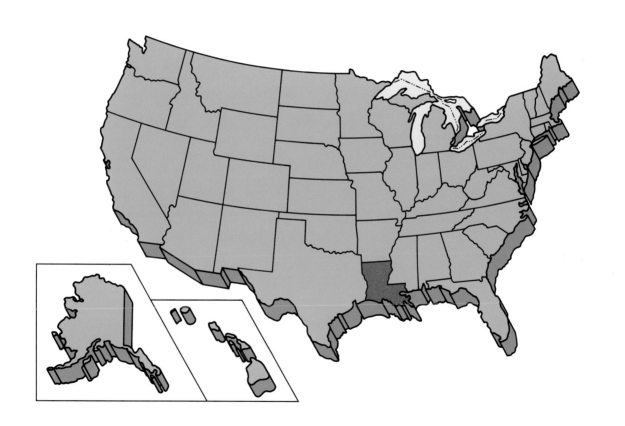

LOUISIANA

Rita C. LaDoux

STATE OF LOUISIANA · UNION JUSTICE · CONFIDENCE

Lerner Publications Company

LIBRARY OF CONGRESS
CATALOGING-IN-PUBLICATION DATA
LaDoux, Rita C.
    Louisiana / Rita C. LaDoux.
      p. cm. — (Hello USA)
    Includes index.
    Summary: Introduces the geography, history, people, industries, and other highlights of Louisiana.
     ISBN 0-8225-2740-5 (lib. bdg.)
    1. Louisiana—Juvenile literature.
    [1. Louisiana.] I. Title. II. Series.
    F369.3.L33 1993
    976.3—dc20   92–13365
                      CIP
                      AC

Manufactured in the United States of America

1 2 3 4 5 6 98 97 96 95 94 93

Cover photograph by Frederica Georgia.

The glossary that begins on page 68 gives definitions of words shown in **bold type** in the text.

 This book is printed on acid-free, recyclable paper.

CONTENTS

❏ The 150,000 alligators in Louisiana have a few special cousins. The state is home to the only known white alligators in the world.

❏ Tabasco pepper sauce was invented and is still made on Avery Island, Louisiana. The company was started in 1868, when Edmund

6

McIlhenny first grew red peppers near his home on the island and bottled the hot, spicy sauce.

❏ The Lake Pontchartrain Causeway is the world's longest bridge. The floating bridge is 29 miles (47 kilometers) long.

❏ French traditions have a strong influence on Louisiana's state government. Unlike other states, Louisiana bases its laws on a code written by the French emperor Napoleon Bonaparte in 1804.

❏ The world's largest private fleet of helicopters takes off once a week from Morgan City, Louisiana. The helicopters carry workers to and from shifts at offshore oil wells.

A Trip Around the State

Louisiana, a southern state, constantly changes its shape. Waves from the Gulf of Mexico, part of the Atlantic Ocean, wash up onto the state's southern shore and carry small chunks of land back to the ocean. At the same time, the Mississippi River carries millions of tons of **sediment** (sand and soil) from the north into Louisiana.

As the Mississippi enters the Gulf, the river drops its load of sediment. The land formed by the buildup of sediment at the mouth of the Mississippi is called a **delta**. The Mississippi Delta makes up about one-fourth of the state.

Trees grow in a bayou, or slow-moving stream.

9

All of Louisiana's rivers make their way to the Gulf of Mexico.

Other rivers have also added land to Louisiana by dropping loads of sediment near the Gulf. In fact, long ago much of what is now Louisiana was actually part of the Gulf of Mexico. But rivers carried enough sediment to fill part of the Gulf.

The Gulf of Mexico washes along Louisiana's entire southern border. The state shares its western border with Texas. The Mississippi River separates much of Louisiana from the state of Mississippi to the east. Arkansas sits to the north. Louisiana itself is divided into three land regions—the Western Coastal Plain, the Mississippi Plain, and the Eastern Coastal Plain.

ARKANSAS

Shreveport

Monroe

Ouachita River

Black River

Mississippi River

Red River

TEXAS

Sabine River

WESTERN
COASTAL
PLAIN

Atchafalaya River

MISSISSIPPI

EASTERN
COASTAL
PLAIN

BATON ROUGE

Lake Charles

Lafayette

Lake Pontchartrain

Mississippi River

New Orleans

MISSISSIPPI
PLAIN

GULF OF MEXICO

LOUISIANA

Regional boundary

Miles
0   30   60

0   30   60
Kilometers

N

The Western Coastal Plain is Louisiana's largest region, covering the entire western half of the state. In the northern part of this region, rivers flow between tree-covered hills. To the south lies a wide band of grassland. South of the grassland are **wetlands**, which include swamps (forested wetlands) and marshes (grassy wetlands). Deposits of oil and natural gas are found in the region's southern marshes and in the north around the city of Shreveport.

From rivers and lakes to marshes and swamps *(left),* Louisiana has a lot of water. Boats head toward the docks in New Orleans *(facing page),* which lies on the banks of the Mississippi River.

The Mississippi Plain stretches along the Mississippi River from Louisiana's northern edge to the Gulf of Mexico. For centuries, the rich soils of this region were built up by sediment that the river dropped each time it flooded. New Orleans and Baton Rouge, the state's two largest cities, are located in the southern third of the Mississippi Plain.

In the southeastern corner of Louisiana lies the Eastern Coastal Plain. Marshes cover this region in the west and south, and prairies blanket the northeast. Once part of Florida, the Eastern Coastal Plain is often called the Florida Parishes. (In Louisiana, counties are called parishes.)

13

Both saltwater and freshwater lakes dot Louisiana. Lake Pontchartrain, north of New Orleans, is the state's largest lake. Louisiana also has many rivers and **bayous,** or slow-moving streams. The state's most important rivers are the Mississippi, the Red, the Atchafalaya, the Ouachita, the Black, and the Sabine.

Warm, moist air travels north from the Gulf of Mexico and gives Louisiana hot and very humid weather. The average summer temperature is a steamy 82° F (28° C), but the thermometer has risen as high as 114° F (46° C). The mild winter temperatures average 55° F (13° C) in the south and 49° F (9° C) in the north.

Each year about 57 inches (145 centimeters) of rain fall on Louisiana, making it one of the wettest states in the country. In the late summer and early fall, hurricanes, or violent storms, form over the ocean. Some of the hurricanes blow in from the Gulf of Mexico and pound Louisiana's coast with heavy rains, high waves, and strong winds.

Summers in Louisiana *(above)* are hot and winters are mild. Snow *(facing page)* doesn't stay on the ground for long.

Nutrias have webbed feet and long tails.

Louisiana's hot, wet weather makes the state a good home for many different types of plants and animals. About half of Louisiana is forested. The state's trees include hickory, magnolia, and pine. Spanish moss, a plant without roots, hangs from bald cypress and oak trees in southern Louisiana. Sweet-smelling flowers such as honeysuckles, camellias, jasmines, and azaleas grow all over the state.

Deer, mink, raccoon, and wild hogs live throughout Louisiana. Alligators and nutrias—small beaverlike animals—thrive in the southern swamps. Oysters and shrimp abound in the state's coastal marshes. The marshes are also the year-round home of birds such as herons, bald eagles, and brown pelicans. Millions of ducks, geese, and other birds spend their winters in Louisiana.

16

Spanish moss hangs from a giant oak tree *(left).* **Flowers such as azaleas** *(inset)* **and magnolias** *(above)*—**the state flower—brighten Louisiana's lush landscape.**

Louisiana's Story

Gumbo—a spicy soup made of okra and a mix of other vegetables, ground sassafras leaves, and meat or seafood—is a specialty of Louisiana's cooks. Like gumbo, the history of the state is a spicy blend of stories and people.

The first people to live in North America were American Indians, or Native Americans. Over time many different Indian groups made their way into what is now Louisiana. By the 1600s as many as 15,000 Indians lived in the area.

The Chitimacha built their villages on the Mississippi Delta. For food, they shot alligators, turtles, and fish with darts from blowguns. The Caddo lived in what is now northwestern Louisiana. These people hollowed out logs to make canoes and built 15-foot-high (5-meter) houses from saplings and grass.

The Natchez, a tribe that lived near the Mississippi River, built their houses out of sun-baked mud and straw. The tribe's king, called the Great Sun, ruled over the Natchez from a village temple. The Natchez and their king didn't know it, but kings in European countries had sent explorers to claim land in North America.

The Great Sun's feet were not supposed to touch the ground, so servants carried the Natchez king everywhere.

La Salle claimed what is now Louisiana for France in 1682.

In 1682 René-Robert Cavelier de La Salle, a French explorer, reached the Gulf of Mexico. He claimed for France the Mississippi River and all the land around all the rivers that flow into it. He named the area Louisiana in honor of Louis XIV, the king of France. Louisiana stretched west from the Mississippi River to the Rocky Mountains, north into what is now Canada, and south to the Gulf.

The French sent soldiers, settlers, food, and supplies to the southern part of their new **colony**, or settlement. Few of the settlers were farmers, so France advertised for farmers in Germany, where many people grew crops for a living.

Germans soon began arriving in Louisiana. They built farms north of the French settlements and began to grow some of the colony's food. Some colonists used black slaves to work on their farms. The slaves were brought to the colony from the West Indies, islands far to the south of Louisiana, and from Africa.

21

The settlers got more food by trading guns, tools, and fabric with the Indians in the area. Unfortunately, the settlers also carried diseases that were deadly to the Indians. These diseases sometimes killed entire tribes.

Soon the settlers wanted to build homes and farms on the homeland of the Natchez Indians. In 1729 the colony's leaders ordered the tribe off its land. The Natchez fought back in a war that became known as the Natchez Revolt. But the French overpowered the tribe. The few Indians who survived were sold into slavery or taken in by other tribes.

France was losing money on Louisiana. The French government had to buy food, guns, and other supplies for the colonists. And Britain, which had a strong army and thousands of colonists in eastern North America, was threatening to take Louisiana away from France. So in 1762 France gave Louisiana to Spain, a country that was a friend to France and an enemy to Britain. Spain had a strong enough army to protect Louisiana from British forces.

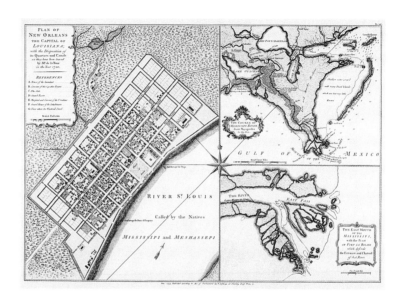

This map of New Orleans was the first map of the city printed in English. Before the 1760s, maps of the area were printed in French.

While under Spanish rule, Louisiana prospered. Settlers living east of the Mississippi sent crops down the river to the growing city of New Orleans, where the crops were shipped to the eastern coast of North America and to Europe. In exchange, manufactured goods were shipped from Europe to New Orleans.

Louisiana's population grew during Spain's rule. New settlers from France joined the **Creoles**—descendants of the earliest French and Spanish settlers, who lived in and around New Orleans. During the mid-1700s, the British forced French settlers out of their homes in Acadia, now part of eastern Canada. Many of these Acadians, called **Cajuns,** moved south to Louisiana, where they could speak French and practice their Catholic religion freely. And thousands of

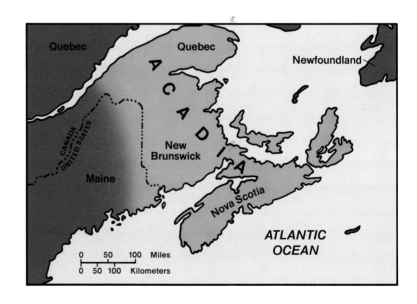

The French colony of Acadia extended from present-day Quebec to eastern Maine and Nova Scotia.

slaves continued to be shipped to Louisiana.

In 1800 Spain agreed to give Louisiana back to France. But just three years later, the French, who still needed money, sold the huge territory to the United States in a deal called the Louisiana Purchase. The U.S. government then divided Louisiana into several smaller territories. On April 30, 1812, one of the territories—Louisiana—became the 18th state of the United States.

Louisiana's state flag shows a pelican—the state bird—feeding her three babies. Because of the brown pelicans that live along the coast, Louisiana is sometimes called the Pelican State.

25

JEAN LAFITTE: Hero or Outlaw?

In 1813, during the War of 1812, Louisiana's governor offered a $500 reward for the capture of a pirate named Jean Lafitte. A Frenchman, Lafitte became well known in New Orleans, where he sold everything from slaves to silks and spices. To get his goods, Lafitte and his crew of ruthless smugglers attacked and took over European ships sailing in the Gulf of Mexico. People in New Orleans were eager to buy the stolen booty, and Lafitte became very rich.

By posting the reward, Louisiana's governor hoped to end Lafitte's raiding. But Great Britain had something else in mind. The British government wanted Jean Lafitte and his men to help capture New Orleans for Great Britain. The British offered Lafitte $30,000 and a pardon for his piracy if he would fight on their side. But Lafitte said no. Instead, he warned the U.S. government of the attack and helped U.S. general Andrew Jackson win the Battle of New Orleans on January 8, 1815. After the war, President James Madison pardoned Lafitte, whose efforts to save New Orleans had made him a war hero.

The white population in the new state included many groups besides Creoles and Cajuns. Some settlers had left more crowded states to the east. Others were **immigrants** from France, Germany, and the West Indies. Most of the black people were slaves, but some black Louisianans were free people of color, a group that included freed slaves and immigrants from the West Indies.

Although they came from many places, people in the new state fell into two main groups—those who had French backgrounds and those who didn't. The Cajuns and Creoles—who lived mainly in southern Louisiana—made up the largest group. They spoke French, had French ancestors, and practiced the Catholic religion. The second group lived mostly in the northern part of the state and in the Florida Parishes. Many of these Louisianans practiced Protestant religions, spoke English, and had British or German ancestors.

Louisiana's immigrants built churches, where they could practice their religions.

27

In the early 1800s, the first steamboat in North America arrived at the port of New Orleans. Steamboats traveled faster and carried more cargo than the old riverboats. Soon more goods were flowing through the city than ever before.

Dock workers unloaded ships that arrived from Europe and the East Coast. Merchants and traders bought the goods and sent them on steamboats up the Mississippi River to be resold. The boats returned to New Orleans filled with grain, cotton, and tobacco. Workers loaded the crops onto ships headed to northern states and to Europe.

New Orleans provided housing and entertainment for the large number of travelers, sailors, and merchants who passed through. The city offered everything from opera and theater to dancing and gambling, or betting on games.

During the 1800s, steamboats carried bales of cotton to market.

Opera houses in New Orleans attracted large audiences.

Free People of Color

In 1820 about 29,000 people lived in New Orleans. Almost half of these residents were black people. As in the rest of Louisiana, many people in New Orleans believed that white people were superior to black people. New Orleans's society was divided basically into three main groups. At the top were white people and at the bottom were slaves. In between were free black people, also called free people of color.

Some slaves were able to gain their freedom. Slave owners, for example, sometimes released slaves who had been hardworking and loyal. Or, if a slave owner had children with one of his slaves, he would usually free the woman and the children. Other slaves were able to buy their freedom, either with money they had earned doing extra work or with help from freed relatives.

Most free people of color in Louisiana lived in New Orleans, where the women could find work as nurses, hairdressers, dressmakers, laundresses, and street vendors. Free black men had jobs as shoemakers, bartenders, laborers, and businessmen.

Free people of color had some rights. They could take an oath in court, make a will, and own property. But they still didn't have as many rights as white people. Free people of color were not allowed to vote, hold public office, or practice law. And whenever they signed official documents—such as wills—they had to add "colored man" or "colored woman" after their signature. Not until 1865, when the 13th Amendment to the U.S. Constitution made slavery illegal, were all African Americans free people of color.

Louisiana's plantation owners lived in large, elegantly furnished homes.

Most slaves lived in small, crowded quarters with dirt floors and no furniture.

Most people in Louisiana lived in the country and worked on farms. Sugarcane was grown in southern Louisiana on **plantations,** or large farms worked by slaves. Plantations farther north grew cotton. Many farmers in southern Louisiana owned plantations, but most of the state's northern farms were small.

Louisiana's planters were not the only ones to use slaves. Plantations all over the South depended on slave labor to make money. But by the 1850s, many people in the United States opposed slavery. Slavery was illegal in Northern states, and many Northern politicians were trying to end slavery in the South.

31

In 1861 Southern states, including Louisiana, withdrew from the United States and formed the Confederate States of America, a separate country where slavery would remain legal. The Union, or Northern states, sent troops to pressure the South to stay in the United States. Soon the Civil War, the war between the North and the South, broke out.

Union troops took over New Orleans in 1862. One year later, they overpowered Confederate forts along the Mississippi River. Union control of the river made it very difficult for Confederates to send food and weapons to their troops.

By 1865, when the Confederacy admitted defeat, homes, barns, roads, and railroads had been destroyed in Louisiana. Many residents had no food, work, or shelter. Slaves had been freed, but most of them had no money or jobs.

To make matters worse, many Northern merchants started using railroads instead of steamboats to ship their goods. The port of New Orleans lost much of its prewar business.

In 1867 U.S. troops from the North moved into Louisiana to oversee **Reconstruction,** or the rebuilding of the South. These troops forced white Louisianans to follow a new U.S. law that gave all black men the right to vote.

African American men, who won the right to vote after the Civil War, register to vote in Caddo Parish.

When the U.S. soldiers left in 1877, some Louisianans were afraid that the vote would give black people too much power. These white Louisianans threatened or attacked blacks who tried to vote. By 1900 Louisiana had passed laws that took the vote away from African American men and from poor white men. The state also passed laws that separated black people from white people in schools, on trains, in restaurants, and at public events such as circuses.

33

By 1900 most Louisianans were still working on farms, but new industries had begun to develop. One was logging. The state's thick forests drew logging companies from northern states, where most of the forests had already been cut. The logging companies built sawmills and hired thousands of Louisianans to chop down the state's trees and cut them into boards.

Louisiana's first oil well was drilled near Jennings in 1901. Soon workers were drilling wells all over the western half of the state. Oil refineries, or factories where oil is cleaned and made into gasoline and other products, were built around Baton Rouge and Shreveport. The refineries employed many more Louisianans.

Oil gushes from a well in Jennings, where oil was first discovered in Louisiana.

34

After trees were chopped down, trains hauled the logs to sawmills.

Huey Long (right) worked to help poor people and was known for saying "Every Man a King."

In the early 1900s, most people in Louisiana lived in areas that could be reached only by dirt roads, which were often muddy and impossible to travel. Many rural, white Louisianans could not get an education because very few schools existed. Even fewer schools were open for black students.

In 1928 a Louisianan named Huey Long ran for governor. Long promised to tax oil and logging companies and to spend the money to help the state's poor people. Long won the election.

To turn his promises into law, Long filled the state government with people who were loyal to him. He soon controlled Louisiana's government completely. He was very popular with people he helped, but he was hated by those who thought he had too much power. Long became a U.S. senator in 1930. He planned to run for president of the United States, but he was assassinated in 1935.

Books for Everyone

Both black and white Louisianans benefited from changes Huey Long made when he was governor. Long built roads, bridges, and hospitals. He expanded library services, provided free textbooks for schoolchildren, and started a program to help adults learn to read and write.

During World War II, Louisiana's factories began building ships for the U.S. Navy.

The outbreak of World War II (1939–1945) brought more jobs and money into the state. Louisiana's oil was needed to fuel tanks and airplanes. And New Orleans bustled as workers loaded ships with supplies needed by the soldiers fighting in Europe.

During the war, the lives of Louisianans improved. And during the **civil rights movement** of the 1960s, black citizens were once again guaranteed the right to vote in Louisiana. African American students also won the right to attend the same schools as white students.

Over the years, many black politicians were elected to government offices, and in 1978 Ernest ("Dutch") Morial became the first black mayor of New Orleans.

Louisiana's oil industry boomed during the 1970s, bringing a lot of money into the state. But by the 1980s, the industry was making less money. State leaders have been trying to attract other businesses to Louisiana so that the state doesn't have to rely only on the success of the oil industry.

Oil is stored in tanks for future use. Only Texas makes more money from oil than Louisiana does.

Timeline:

- **10,000 B.C.** — Native Americans enter what is now Louisiana
- **A.D.1682** — La Salle claims Louisiana for France
- **1729** — Natchez Revolt
- **1803** — Louisiana Purchase
- **1812** — Louisiana becomes the 18th state

Louisiana is also working to protect the state's natural environment. Each year the state loses miles of coastal wetlands. To help stop this loss, Louisianans started the Wetlands Conservation and Restoration Fund in 1989. This fund provides money for projects that will help save coastal wetlands. Although problems remain, Louisianans are working together to try to solve them.

1861 Louisiana joins the Confederate States of America

1901 Workers drill Louisiana's first oil well

1928 Huey Long is elected governor

1960 Black students and white students begin attending the same elementary schools

Voters in New Orle... city's first Africa...

In 1989 Louisianans set up
Wetlands Conservation and
Restoration Fund to protec...
state's wetlands.

42

Living and Working in Louisiana

The French, Spanish, and African peoples of Louisiana have given the state a flavor all its own. European-style buildings and regional foods and music reflect the state's unique character.

Northern and southern Louisianans still have their differences, but the state is no longer split between English and French speakers. Almost 70 percent of Louisianans are white. Black Louisianans make up about 30 percent of the population. Smaller groups of people in the state include Latinos, Native Americans, and Asian Americans.

Native Americans make up less than 1 percent of Louisiana's population.

43

New Orleans is known for its French-style architecture.

Almost 4.5 million people live in Louisiana, mostly in urban areas. The largest city in Louisiana is New Orleans. Baton Rouge, the next largest, is the state capital. Shreveport and Monroe are in the north. Lafayette and Lake Charles, in the south, are not far from the Gulf coast.

Every year the cities and towns of Louisiana come alive with festivals. Ruston celebrates peaches in June, Farmerville honors watermelons in July, and Colfax features pecans in November.

But the state's most famous festival is Mardi Gras, held in New

Orleans and other towns in southern Louisiana. Mardi Gras is a festival held on the day before the beginning of Lent, a period of fasting before Easter. In the weeks leading up to Mardi Gras, musicians and wildly dressed people parade down the streets on floats and dance at costume balls.

Festivals also celebrate the music of Louisiana. Marthaville hosts the Louisiana State Fiddling Contest each April. New Orleans, the birthplace of jazz, holds the Jazz and Heritage Festival each spring. Jazz artists perform nightly at Preservation Hall in New Orleans.

Louisianans use their imagination to dress up for Mardi Gras.

At Lafayette's Festivals Acadiens held each September, musicians play Cajun tunes. Another type of music native to Louisiana is zydeco, which combines rock and roll with Cajun and African American sounds.

Along with Louisiana's unique music comes its spicy and unusual food. Restaurants feature local shrimp, crab, oysters, crayfish, and fish in dishes such as jambalaya (spicy rice with seafood or meat) and gumbo.

A father and daughter peel crayfish at a festival in Shreveport that honors the lobsterlike shellfish.

Musicians play toe-tapping Cajun music *(above)* in Lafayette. Jazz musicians *(right)* are a common sight on the streets of New Orleans.

A young boater paddles a pirogue, or canoe, across a small lake.

Football fans go wild in the Superdome, home of the New Orleans Saints—Louisiana's only professional sports team. Every New Year's Day, two of the best college football teams in the nation clash in the Sugar Bowl game at the Superdome.

Louisianans play sports as well as watch sports. Rodeos, horse races, and pirogue (canoe) races draw participants and fans from around the state and the nation. Many people enjoy fishing in the state's bayous, in its lakes, and in the Gulf of Mexico. Bayou cruises and swamp tours, which are offered throughout the state, give visitors a chance to see unusual birds, alligators, and other wetland wildlife.

Louisianans work at many different kinds of jobs. Most—about 75 percent—work at service jobs. People with service jobs help other people or businesses. Service workers include teachers, bankers, waitpeople, and government workers.

A waitperson in the historic French Quarter of New Orleans is one of the city's many service workers.

Shipping is an important source of service jobs in Louisiana. Barges loaded with grain, oil, and chemicals travel down the state's rivers to the port of New Orleans. Ship pilots bring cargo into New Orleans from around the world. Workers called stevedores load and unload the barges and ships, and traders buy and sell the goods. Truck drivers deliver some of the goods to local stores, and salespeople sell the items to customers.

Only 3 percent of Louisiana's workers earn money from agriculture, but farmers plant crops on about one-third of the state's land. In southern Louisiana, farmers grow rice in flooded fields. In the valleys of the Red and Mississippi rivers, farmers raise soybeans, cotton, and sugarcane. In northern Louisiana, pine and oak trees are planted for future logging. And in ponds throughout the state, farmers raise crayfish and catfish to sell to restaurants and grocery stores.

A ship *(left)* on the Mississippi River brings cargo to New Orleans, one of the busiest ports in the United States. Some of Louisiana's logs and lumber *(above)* are shipped out of the state.

Louisiana's most important sea-foods—shrimp and oysters—come from the Gulf of Mexico. Louisiana's fishers bring in nearly one-fourth of all the seafood caught in the United States.

The Gulf of Mexico is also rich in oil. Each year, workers pump millions of barrels of oil and natural gas in the Gulf and throughout the state. Louisiana supplies about one-fourth of the oil and one-third of the natural gas mined in the United States. Only 4 percent of working Louisianans have mining jobs, but these people earn about 17 percent of the state's money.

More than 10 percent of Louisiana's workers have jobs in manufacturing. They process products

A fisher shows off the day's shrimp catch.

from the state's farming, logging, fishing, and mining industries into finished goods. People at food-processing plants pack seafood. Mill workers cut trees into lumber or grind wood into pulp for paper.

Workers at refineries mix oil products with other chemicals to make fertilizers and plastics. And Louisiana's shipbuilders make boats that transport these products to markets all over the world.

Workers *(left)* drill for oil in the Gulf of Mexico. The oil is sent to refineries *(above)* in cities such as Baton Rouge and Westlake.

53

Protecting the Environment

Louisiana's wetlands are among the state's most valuable natural resources. More than 1 million Louisianans earn their living from wetlands, and almost 1.5 million of the state's residents make their homes in wetland areas. But Louisiana is losing many of its coastal wetlands to **erosion**, a process in which water washes away loose soil.

The marshes that are eroding have been very important to the state's economy. People catch fish and shellfish that lay eggs in the coastal marshes. Louisiana's seafood brings almost $700 million into the state every year. In the state's swamps, trappers catch nutrias and sell their skins. Hunters, fishers, and tourists in wetland areas spend millions of dollars at Louisiana's restaurants, motels, and stores each year.

Alligators *(facing page)* **live in Louisiana's coastal wetlands** *(above).*

Coastal marshes are very important to wildlife and plants, too. Millions of ducks and geese depend on Louisiana's marshes for food and shelter in the winter. Other birds rest and feed in the marshes while traveling to their winter or summer homes. Some types of plants in Louisiana's marshes cannot grow anywhere else in the United States.

Coastal marshes also protect inland towns from the full force of hurricanes. As hurricane winds pass over the marshes, the storms slow down, causing less damage when they finally hit inland towns. Marshes also hold some of the water that would otherwise flood coastal towns when storms strike.

The ocean waves that lap against Louisiana's coast have eroded

marshes naturally for thousands of years. But the Mississippi River also dropped tons of soil all along its banks each time it flooded. The sediment was then carried by smaller rivers and streams into the marshes, where the soil settled, repairing the damage caused by the ocean.

In the late 1800s, the marshes started eroding faster than they could be rebuilt. As people built homes and farms along the Mississippi, they also built **levees**, or walls that keep rivers from flooding. No flooding meant no sediment to replace marshland that had washed away.

The levees also made the river straighter, which caused it to flow faster. The Mississippi River now flows so fast into the Gulf of Mexico that much of its sediment gets carried out to deep Gulf waters instead of settling in marshes.

Many Canada geese *(facing page)* **spend the winter in Louisiana's marshes** *(right).*

Mining practices also cause coastal marshes to erode. Much of Louisiana's oil and natural gas is found in coastal marshes. To get to these fuels, workers dig canals through marshes.

When storms blow water toward the coast, the long, straight canals let the seawater travel far into the marshes. The salty Gulf water kills plants that can only grow in the fresh water of the marshes. Without plant roots to hold soil in place, waves wash the soil away. The water then becomes too deep for marsh plants and animals, and the marsh becomes an open pond or lake.

Louisiana is losing at least 40 square miles (104 sq km) of coastal marshes a year. At that rate, in about 50 years Louisiana will lose a piece of coastland bigger than the state of Rhode Island. To try to save this area, Louisianans started the Wetlands Conservation and Restoration Fund in 1989. This fund gives millions of dollars each year to projects that will protect Louisiana's wetlands.

58

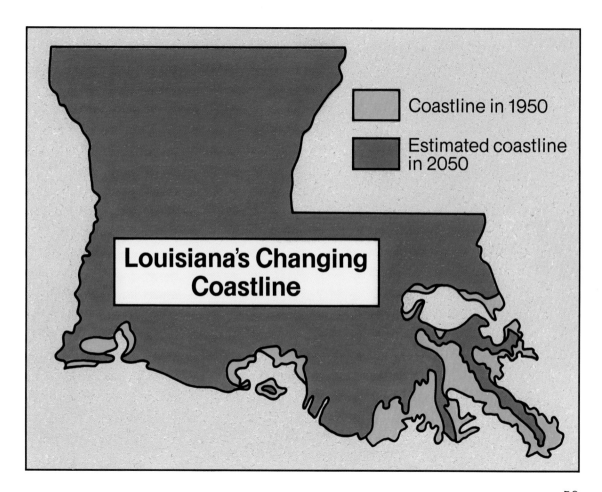

Louisiana's Changing Coastline

Coastline in 1950

Estimated coastline in 2050

To help create new marshes, workers build fences from Christmas trees, which trap soil needed for plants to grow.

In one of the programs paid for by the trust fund, workers have cut into levees along the Mississippi River to let water and soil flood the wetlands. In another program, two rows of fences are built close together along the coast. Dead Christmas trees are then stacked between the fences. When water moves through the fences, the trees break the waves and hold the soil. The deposits of soil become islands. Plants begin to grow on the islands, and eventually the islands become a new marsh.

When mining companies are done using a canal, they now must plug it at both ends or fill it so that salt water cannot get into the canal. Sometimes workers plant marsh grasses on the former canal. The roots of the plants slow erosion by holding soil in place.

All of these efforts have saved or rebuilt marshes, but erosion continues. As Louisianans keep finding ways to restore marshes, they give coastal marshes a better chance to survive.

Workers plant grasses to help prevent marsh soil from eroding.

Louisiana's Famous People

CLEMENTINE HUNTER ◄

Jose Ruiz De Rivera (1904–1985), a sculptor from West Baton Rouge, Louisiana, created artworks by heating and molding thick steel rods. He formed rounded pieces, buffed them to a shine, and placed them on turning bases. De Rivera's work is displayed in some of the country's best-known museums.

Clementine Hunter (1887–1988) grew up on a plantation near New Orleans. Hunter's simple and colorful oil paintings—done on cardboard, plywood, and brown paper bags—show the daily lives of black plantation workers.

TERRY BRADSHAW ►

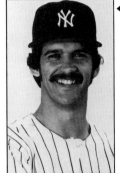

◄ **RON GUIDRY**

ATHLETES

Terry Bradshaw (born 1948), from Shreveport, Louisiana, played football for the Pittsburgh Steelers from 1970 to 1984. The popular quarterback led the team to win four Super Bowls.

Ron Guidry (born 1950) pitched for the New York Yankees baseball team. In 1978 he won 25 games, winning the Cy Young Award for best pitcher in the American League. Guidry, born in Lafayette, Louisiana, is called Louisiana Lightning for his fast pitches.

Mel Ott (1909–1958) played baseball with the New York Giants from 1926 to 1947. Ott, who was born in Gretna, Louisiana, hit 511 home runs during his career. He was elected to the National Baseball Hall of Fame in 1951.

MEL OTT ►

Bill Russell (born 1934) is from Monroe, Louisiana. Known for his defense skills, Russell played center for the Boston Celtics from 1956 to 1969. He became the first black coach in the National Basketball Association and was elected to the National Basketball Hall of Fame in 1975.

▲ BILL RUSSELL

JAZZ ARTISTS

Louis Armstrong (1900–1971) was a jazz musician and band-leader. Born in New Orleans, Armstrong was known as a world-class trumpet player. He became so popular that postal carriers delivered letters addressed only to Louis Armstrong, Mr. Jazz, U.S.A.

◄ LOUIS ARMSTRONG

WYNTON MARSALIS ▼

Wynton Marsalis (born 1961) is a trumpet player from New Orleans who plays both classical and jazz music. In 1984 he became the first musician to win Grammy Awards for his recordings of both types of music.

Jelly Roll Morton (1885–1941) was born in Gulfport, Louisiana. Morton played the piano and wrote and arranged music for jazz bands. Morton is known for many compositions, including "Jelly Roll Blues" and "King Porter Stomp."

OUTLAWS

Jean Lafitte (1780?–1825?) was a French pirate based in New Orleans. During the War of 1812, British officers asked him to help attack New Orleans. Instead Lafitte aided the U.S. side. After the war, Lafitte went back to robbing ships until he disappeared around 1825.

63

Lee Harvey Oswald (1939–1963) was born in New Orleans. Many people believe he assassinated President John F. Kennedy in 1963. Two days after Kennedy died, Oswald himself was shot and killed while under arrest for the murder of the president.

◀ LEE HARVEY OSWALD

POLITICAL & SOCIAL LEADERS

Huey Long (1893–1935) and **Earl Long** (1895–1960) were born near Winnfield, Louisiana. Huey served as the state's governor from 1928 to 1932. For the next three years, he served as one of Louisiana's U.S. senators. Huey's brother Earl was the state's governor three different times in the 1940s and 1950s. The Long family was very powerful in Louisiana's politics, making friends as well as fierce enemies.

▲ EARL LONG ▲ HUEY LONG

Edward Perkins (born 1928) became the first black U.S. ambassador to the country of South Africa in 1986. After his term, Perkins was appointed director general of the Foreign Service and director of personnel for the Department of State. Perkins was born in Sterlington, Louisiana.

EDWARD ▶
PERKINS

SCIENTIST

Jerome Hunsaker (1886–1984), from Creston, Louisiana, designed and built aircraft. In 1914 he built the first working wind tunnel, which tests the effects of wind pressure on airplanes in flight.

64

◀ HARRY
CONNICK, JR.

Harry Connick, Jr. (born 1968), started playing the piano at the age of three. Born in New Orleans, Connick is now a world-famous pianist and singer with his own 30-piece orchestra. He has won two Grammy Awards and has also acted in movies.

Fats Domino (born 1928), from New Orleans, sings music that is a blend of the blues and rock and roll. In 1956 he recorded the hit song "Blueberry Hill," which is still popular.

Hank Williams, Jr. (born 1949), has been a well-known country-western singer since the 1960s. In 1987 and 1988 he was named the Country Music Entertainer of the Year. Williams is from Shreveport, Louisiana.

HANK ▶
WILLIAMS, JR.

▲ FATS
DOMINO

◀ WILLIAM
JOYCE

▲ TRUMAN
CAPOTE

Truman Capote (1924–1984) was born in New Orleans. A great storyteller during his lifetime, Capote is known for novels such as *In Cold Blood* and *Breakfast at Tiffany's,* both of which were made into movies in the 1960s.

William Joyce (born 1957), from Shreveport, Louisiana, writes and illustrates children's stories. His books include *Dinosaur Bob and His Adventures with the Family Lazardo, A Day with Wilbur Robinson,* and *George Shrinks.*

Facts-at-a-Glance

Nickname: Pelican State
Songs: "Give Me Louisiana" and
 "You Are My Sunshine"
Motto: Union, Justice, and Confidence
Flower: magnolia
Tree: bald cypress
Bird: brown pelican

Population: 4,219,973*
Rank in population, nationwide: 21st
Area: 51,843 sq mi (134,273 sq km)
Rank in area, nationwide: 31st
Date and ranking of statehood:
 April 30, 1812, the 18th state
Capital: Baton Rouge
Major cities (and populations*):
 New Orleans (496,938), Baton Rouge
 (219,531), Shreveport (198,525), Lafayette
 (94,440), Kenner (72,033)
U.S. senators: 2
U.S. representatives: 7
Electoral votes: 9

Places to visit: French Quarter in New Orleans, Oaklawn Plantation near Natchitoches, Original Swamp Gardens in Morgan City, Louisiana Purchase Gardens and Zoo in Monroe, Tabasco Pepper Sauce Factory on Avery Island

Annual events: Mardi Gras in New Orleans and other cities (Feb./March), Holiday in Dixie in Shreveport (April), World Champion Pirogue Races in Lafitte (June), Frog Festival in Rayne (Sept.), Louisiana State Fair in Shreveport (Oct.)

* 1990 census

| **Average January temperature:** 50° F (10° C) | **Average July temperature:** 82° F (28° C) |

Natural resources: oil, natural gas, salt, lumber, soil, sulfur

Agricultural products: soybeans, cotton, rice, sugarcane, corn, strawberries, sweet potatoes, beef cattle, dairy cattle

Manufactured goods: fertilizers, paint, plastics, food products, ships, paper products

ENDANGERED SPECIES
Mammals—silver-haired bat
Birds—brown pelican, crested caracara, interior least tern, willow flycatcher, worm-eating warbler
Reptiles—loggerhead turtle, stripeneck musk turtle, gopher tortoise, black pine snake
Fish—lake sturgeon, gulf sturgeon, pallid sturgeon
Plants—hairy lipfern, swamp thistle, gummy lovegrass, wahoo, old field sneezeweed, june grass, wiry witchgrass, turkey oak

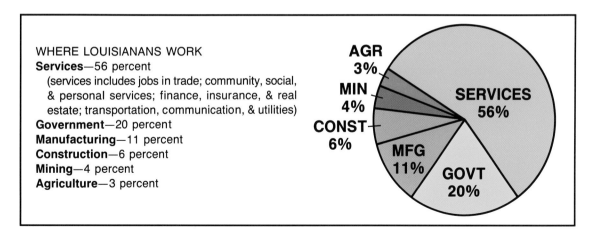

WHERE LOUISIANANS WORK
Services—56 percent
   (services includes jobs in trade; community, social, & personal services; finance, insurance, & real estate; transportation, communication, & utilities)
Government—20 percent
Manufacturing—11 percent
Construction—6 percent
Mining—4 percent
Agriculture—3 percent

AGR
3%
MIN
4%
CONST
6%
MFG
11%
GOVT
20%
SERVICES
56%

Atchafalaya (uh-chaf-uh-LY-uh)

Baton Rouge (BAT-uhn ROOZH)

Caddo (KAD-oh)

Cajun (KAY-juhn)

Chitimacha (chihd-uh-MAH-shuh)

Creole (KREE-ohl)

Lafayette (laf-ee-EHT)

Mardi Gras (MAHRD-ee grah)

Natchez (NACH-ehz)

New Orleans (noo AWR-luhnz)

Ouachita (WAHSH-uh-taw)

Pontchartrain (PAHN-chuhr-trayn)

Shreveport (SHREEV-pohrt)

Glossary

bayou A marshy or very slow-moving body of water.

Cajun A person whose French-speaking ancestors came to Louisiana from Acadia in the 1750s. Acadia covered parts of eastern Canada and Maine.

civil rights movement A movement to gain equal rights, or freedoms, for all citizens—regardless of race, religion, or sex.

colony A territory ruled by a country some distance away.

Creole A person whose ancestors came to Louisiana from France or Spain. Creoles also include people who have a heritage of French or Spanish and African roots.

delta   A triangular piece of land at the mouth of a river. A delta is formed from soil deposited by the river.

erosion   The wearing away of the earth's surface by the forces of water, wind, or ice.

immigrant   A person who moves into a foreign country and settles there.

levee   A wall built along a riverbank to prevent the river from flooding. Levees are usually made by piling up sandbags and dirt.

plantation   A large estate, usually in a warm climate, on which crops are grown by workers who live on the estate. In the past, plantation owners usually used slave labor.

Reconstruction   The period from 1865 to 1877 during which the U.S. government brought the Southern states back into the Union after the Civil War.

Before rejoining the Union, a Southern state had to pass a law allowing black men to vote. Places destroyed in the war were rebuilt and industries were developed.

sediment   Solid materials—such as soil, sand, and minerals—that are carried into a body of water by wind, ice, or running water.

wetland   A swamp, marsh, or other low, wet area that often borders a river, lake, or ocean. Wetlands support many different kinds of plants and animals.

Index

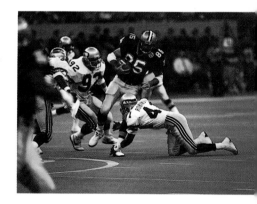

Acknowledgments:

Maryland Cartographics, Inc., pp. 2, 11; Frederica Georgia, pp. 2–3, 6, 13, 15, 17 (left), 27, 42, 47 (left), 48, 49, 52, 55, 69; George Karn, p. 7; © James Blank/Root Resources, pp. 8–9, 50–51, 53 (right); Dianne Lindstedt, Louisiana Geological Survey, LSU, pp. 10, 45; David Kelley, p. 12; Lynda Richards, pp. 14, 17 (right & inset), 31 (both), 46, 47 (right), 51 (right), 56; Kay Shaw Photography, pp. 16, 44; The Historic New Orleans Collection, Museum/Research Center, pp. 19 (Acc. #1980.205.33), 20–21 (Acc. #1970.1), 29 (Acc. #1951.72); Historic Urban Plans/Library of Congress, p. 23; Independent Picture Service, pp. 26, 63 (top), 64 (middle left); Photograph Collection, Louisiana Division, New Orleans Public Library, pp. 28, 34, 36, 38; Louisiana State Museum, p. 30; LSU-Shreveport Archives, p. 33, 35, 37; Charles F. Swenson, p. 39; Karen Westphal, Louisiana Geological Survey, LSU, p. 41; Thomas Ritter/Monroe-West Monroe Convention & Visitors Bureau, p. 43; Diane Cooper, p. 53 (left), 54; Gary Peterson, Coastal Ecology Laboratory, LSU, p. 57; Coastal Restoration Division, Louisiana DNR, p. 61; Collection of Thomas N. Whitehead, p. 62 (top left); Pittsburgh Steelers, p. 62 (top right); New York Yankees, p. 62 (bottom left); National Baseball Library, Cooperstown, NY, p. 62 (bottom right); TV Times, p. 63 (middle); Columbia Records, p. 63 (bottom); UPI/Bettmann, p. 64 (top); Louisiana State Library, Louisiana Section, p. 64 (middle right); U.S. Mission to the United Nations, p. 64 (bottom); Hollywood Book & Poster Co., p. 65 (top left & right); Warner Brothers Records, p. 65 (middle); © Nancy Crampton, p. 65 (bottom left); Kathryn Clay Gaiennie, p. 65 (bottom right); Tim Alexander/New Orleans Saints, p. 7.